E S T A T E   P U B L I C A T I O N S

STIRLING · ALLOA
BRIDGE OF ALLAN · DUNBLANE

GW01157611

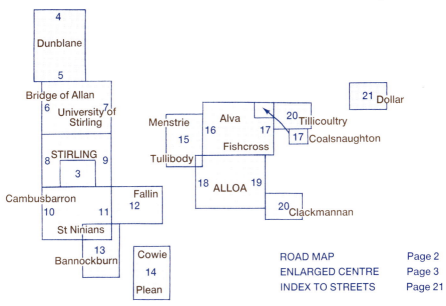

4 Dunblane

5 Bridge of Allan

6 University of Stirling   7

Menstrie   Alva   16   17   20 Tillicoultry   21 Dollar

15   Fishcross   17 Coalsnaughton

8 STIRLING 9   Tullibody

3

Cambusbarron   Fallin   18 ALLOA 19   20 Clackmannan

10   11   12

St Ninians

13 Bannockburn   Cowie   14   Plean

ROAD MAP	Page 2
ENLARGED CENTRE	Page 3
INDEX TO STREETS	Page 21

Every effort has been made to verify the accuracy of information in this book but the publishers cannot accept responsibility for expense or loss caused by an error or omission. Information that will be of assistance to the user of the maps will be welcomed.

The representation of a road, track or footpath on the maps in this atlas is no evidence of the existence of a right of way.

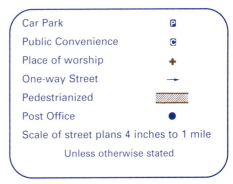

Car Park	🅿
Public Convenience	Ⓒ
Place of worship	✛
One-way Street	→
Pedestrianized	▨
Post Office	●

Scale of street plans 4 inches to 1 mile

Unless otherwise stated

Street plans prepared and published by ESTATE PUBLICATIONS, Bridewell House, TENTERDEN, KENT, and based upon the ORDNANCE SURVEY maps with the sanction of the Controller of H. M. Stationery Office.

Maps drawn by C. Wheeler

The Publishers acknowledge the co-operation of Stirling C.R.C. and Clackmannan D.C.

© Estate Publications 476A   ISBN 0 86084 589 3   Crown Copyright reserved

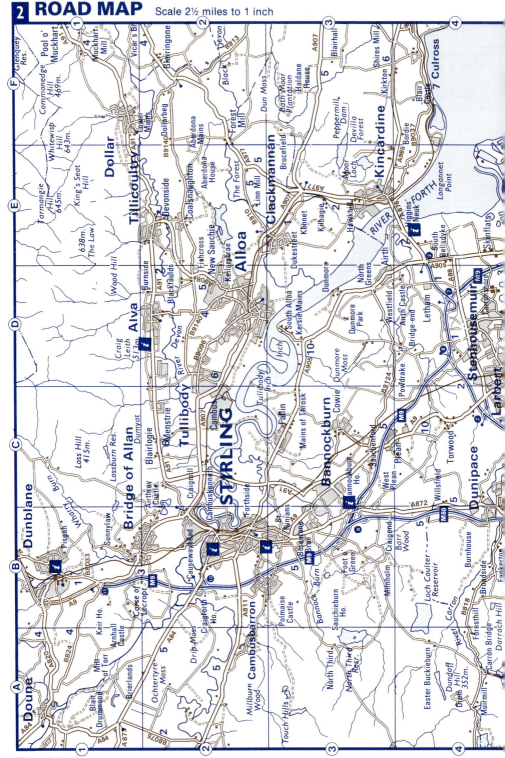

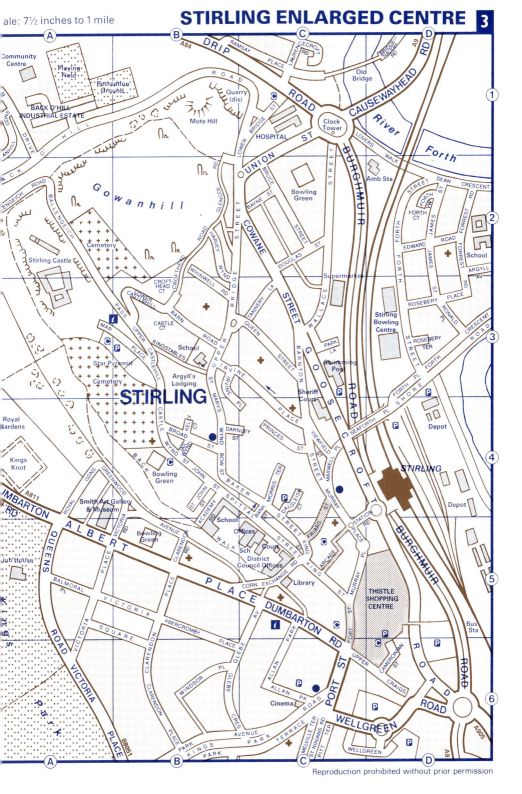

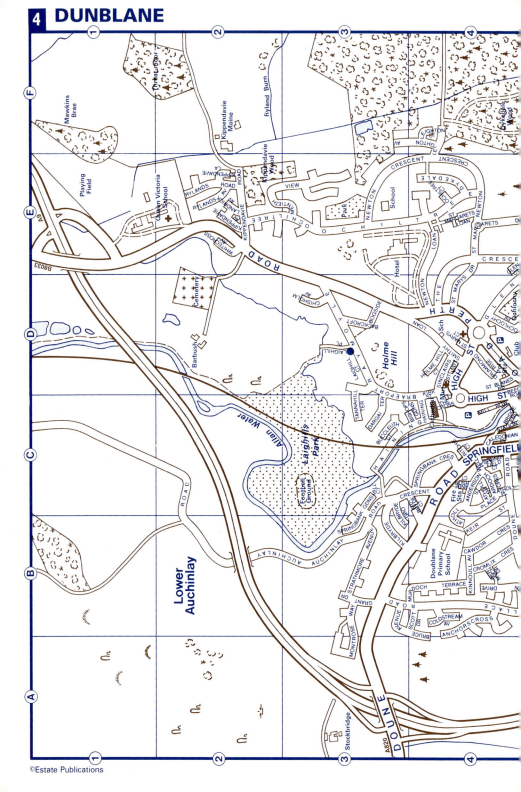

4 DUNBLANE

©Estate Publications

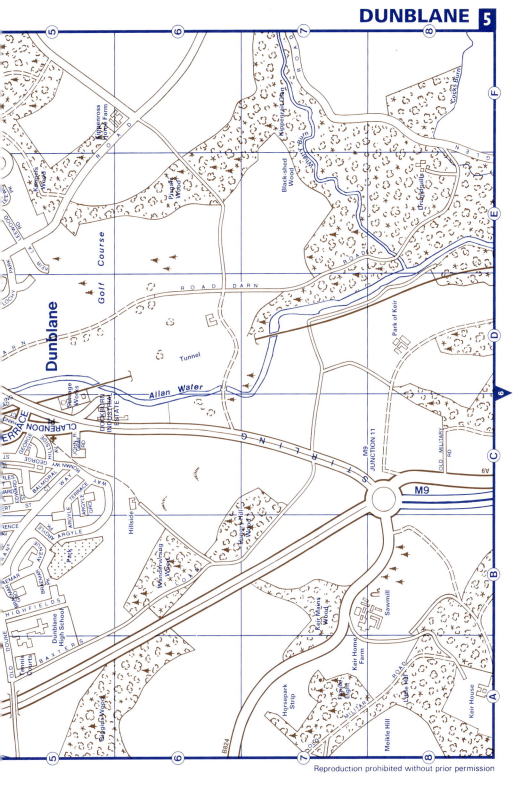

Dunblane

Golf Course

Kippenross Home Farm

Kippenross Glen

Black-shed Wood

Pisgah Wood

Glen

Cocks Burn

Kempers Wood

Drumdruills

Park of Keir

ROAD DARN

Tunnel

Allan Water

Sewage Works

DOCKBURN INDUSTRIAL ESTATE

CLARENDON PLACE

TERRACE

M9 JUNCTION 11

OLD MILITARY RD

A9

STIRLING

M9

Hillside

Huggill Hill Wood

Winnelvvraag Wood

Park

Argyle

Dunblane High School

Tennis Courts

BAXTERS

Keir Mains Wood

Sawmill

Keir House

Keir Home Farm

Little Hill

Flying Eight

Horsepark Strip

Meikle Hill

MILITARY ROAD

Edgieds Wood

B824

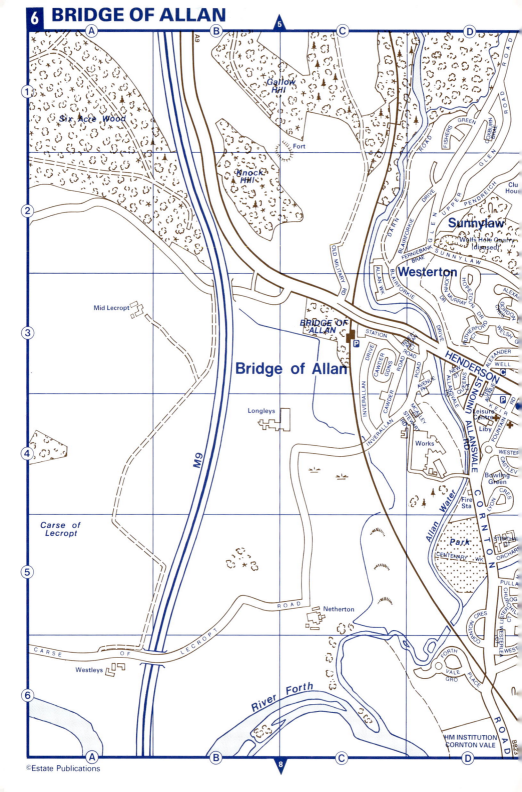

Six Acre Wood

Gallow Hill

Fort

Knock Hill

FISHERS GREEN

OXBURN BRAE

GLEN ROAD

UPPER GLEN ROAD

PENDREICH

Clu Hous

Sunnylaw

Wolfs Hole Quarry (disused)

DARN DRIVE

BLAIRFORKIE BRAE

FERNIEBANK BRAE

SUNNYLAW ROAD

Westerton

ALLAN WK

BLAIRFORKIE

OLD MILITARY RD

JOHN MURRAY DR

HOPETON DR

RUTHERFORD

WELSH G

ALEXA

GORDON CRES

Mid Lecropt

BRIDGE OF ALLAN

STATION

HENDERSON

ALEXANDER WELL

Bridge of Allan

CAWDER DRIVE

QUEENS

P

CAWDER GDNS

STATION ROAD

FOUNTAIN ROAD

AVENUE

ALLANVALE

NEW

ALBERT

ALEXANDRA

UNION ST

Longleys

INVERALLAN DRIVE

INVERALLAN ROAD

MCALEY

STEWART

PK

ALLANVALE RD

Leisure Centre

KEIR

FOUNTAIN

P

Liby

Works

CASTLEV

WESTEF

Bowling Green

CORNTON

LINTON CRES

Fire Sta

STRATH

Carse of Lecropt

Allan Water

Park

CENTENARY WK

ORCHARD

PULLA

M9

A9

River Forth

ROAD

Netherton

CORNTON

CONNOCH CRES

CHURCHILL

LISTER

WESTERLE

WEST

FORTH VALE GRO

PLACE

CARSE OF LECROPT ROAD

Westleys

HM INSTITUTION CORNTON VALE

ROAD

B823

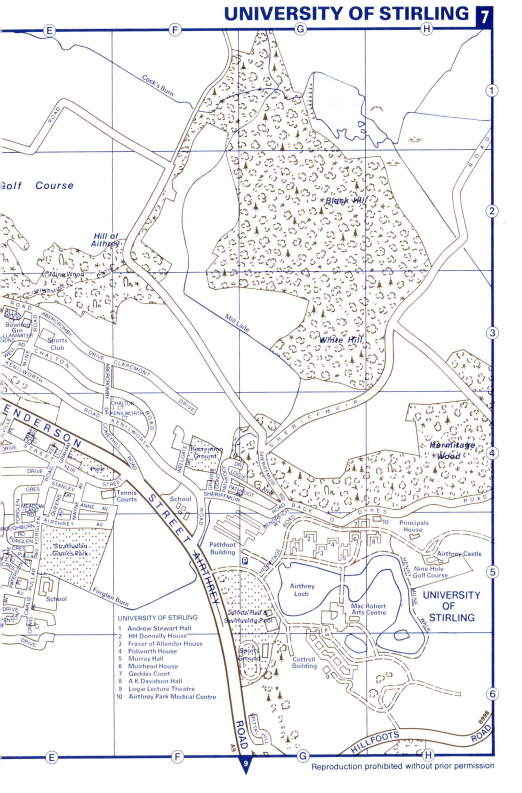

E F G H

1
2
3
4
5
6

Cock's Burn

Golf Course

Hill of Aithrey

Black Hill

Ming Wood

ALLAN WOOD

Bowling Grn

LLANWATER GDNS

Sports Club

WELL RD

KENILWORTH

MINE ROAD

CHALTON

ABERCROMBY

DRIVE

ABERCROMBY

CLAREMONT

DRIVE

CHALTON CT

KENILWORTH

DR

ROAD

KENILWORTH

CONEYHILL ROAD

Mill Lade

White Hill

SHERIFFMUIR

Hermitage Wood

HENDERSON

VILLE

DRIVE

STREET

KEIR

ROAD

GRAHAM

KEIR

STANLEY

QUEENS DR

MAYNE

ANNE AV

AIRTHREY AV

Park

STREET

Tennis Courts

School

Recreation Ground

WELLGATE

GRANGE GDNS

DR

PATHFOOT

PATHFOOT

SHERIFFMUIR

LOGIE

DR LOGIE

SHERIFFMUIR RD

LANE

ROAD BACK O DYKES

BENDRICK WD

ROAD

10

Principals House

FORGLEN

MEADOW LAND RD

FORGLEN CRES

LOUGHBURN RD

FORGLEN

HEME CRES

PULLAR

CRES

PATERSON

CARLIE PULLAR

CRAIG

AV

AV

DRIVE

HENSON

Strathallan Games Park

School

Forglen Burn

STREET AIRTHREY

Pathfoot Building

P

Sports Ground

Sports Hall & Swimming Pool

Airthrey Loch

1

2

3

4

5

6

7

8

9

Mac Robert Arts Centre

Cottrell Building

HERMITAGE

HENRY MILNE WALK

Airthrey Castle

Nine-Hole Golf Course

UNIVERSITY OF STIRLING

UNIVERSITY OF STIRLING

1   Andrew Stewart Hall
2   HH Donnelly House
3   Fraser of Allander House
4   Polworth House
5   Murray Hall
6   Muirhead House
7   Geddes Court
8   A K Davidson Hall
9   Logie Lecture Theatre
10   Airthrey Park Medical Centre

ROAD

SPITTAL HILL

A9

HILLFOOTS

ROAD

B998

9

E F G H

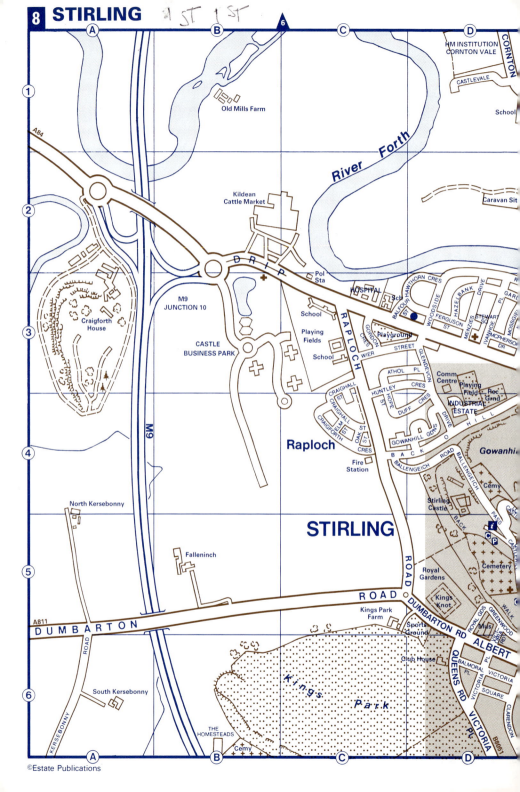

8 STIRLING

A811 / **A84** / **M9** / **M9 JUNCTION 10**

River Forth

Old Mills Farm

HM INSTITUTION CORNTON VALE

CORNTON

CASTLEVALE

School

Caravan Sit

Kildean Cattle Market

DRIP

Pol Sta

HOSPITAL

Sch

BALFOUR ST
HAWTHORN CRES
WOODSIDE
FERGUSON ST
MENZIES ST
HAZELBANK PL
VAN IVANJOE
STEWART ST
MCPHERSON DR
GARL
MOSSGIE

School

Playground

STREET

RAPLOCH

Playing Fields

School

GORDON CRES
WIER

ATHOL PL
GLENDEVON CRES
Comm Centre
Playing Field
Rec Grnd

HUNTLEY ST
HOPE ST
DUFF CRES
INDUSTRIAL ESTATE

Craigforth House

CASTLE BUSINESS PARK

CRAIGHALL ST
CRAIGFORTH CRES
OAK ST
GOWANHILL GDNS

DRIVE
HILL

Gowanhi

BACK

Raploch

BALLENGEICH

Fire Station

Stirling Castle

Cemy

BALLENGEICH ROAD

PASS

CASTLE

i
C P

North Kersebonny

STIRLING

Falleninch

Cemetery

Gowanhi

BACK

Royal Gardens

ROAD

Kings Knot

DUMBARTON RD

Mus

ALBERT

ROYAL GDS
GREENWOOD
WALK

Club House

BALMORAL PL
VICTORIA

QUEENS RD

VICTORIA SQUARE

A811

DUMBARTON **ROAD**

Kings Park Farm

Sports Ground

VICTORIA

CLARENDON

B8051

ROAD
KERSEBONNY

South Kersebonny

THE HOMESTEADS

Cemy

Kings Park

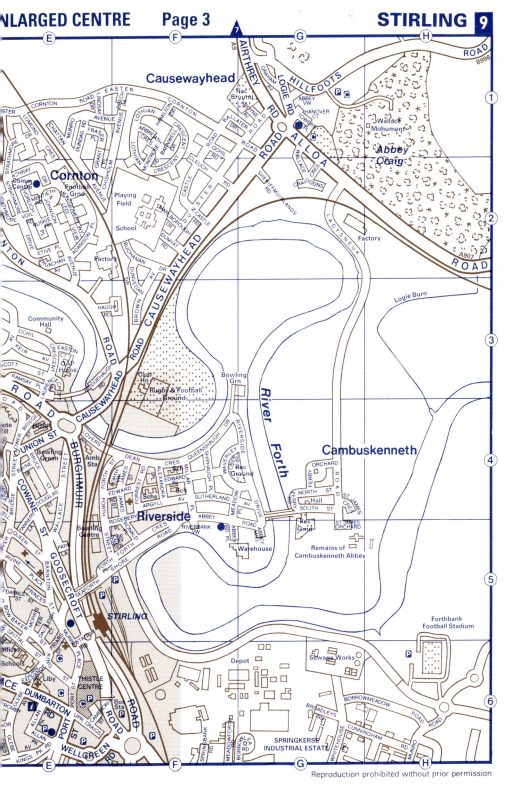

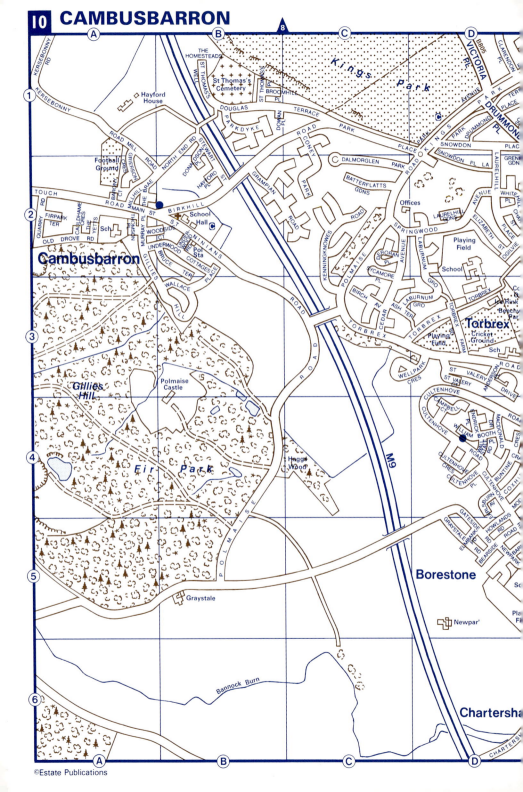

10 CAMBUSBARRON

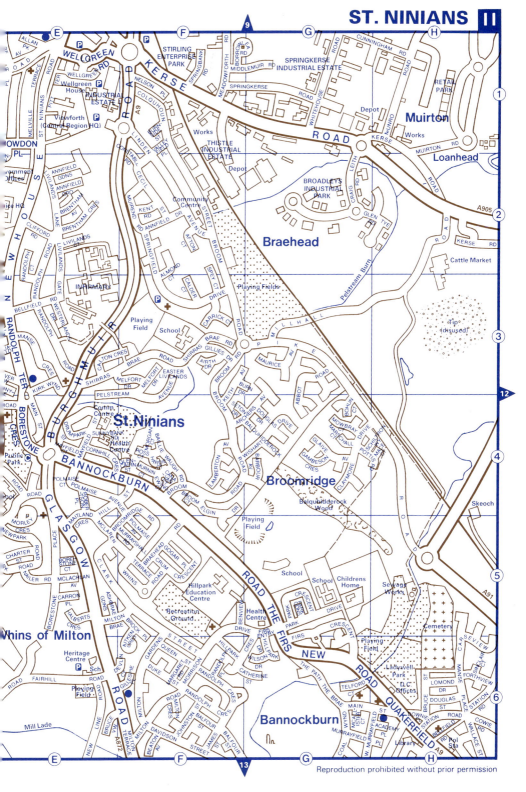

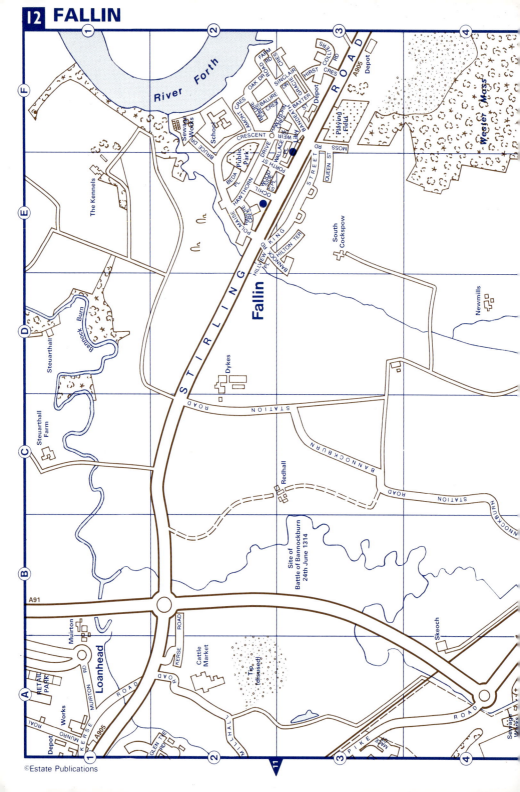

12 FALLIN

River Forth

Weester Moss

A905

Depot

SHS

COLL RD

HIRST CRES

SINCLAIR

OXEN DR RD

FARM

CRES

OAK DR

ROSEBALURE PL

CRES

LANGDYKE

BAXTER

PL

WEIR

BANNER

CRESCENT

School

BRUCE DR

Sewage Works

The Kennels

Bannock Burn

Steuarthall

Steuarthall Farm

BEDA PL

Public Park

HAWTHORN CRES

POLMAISE CRES

OCHIL CRES

DRIVE

FORTH ST

WALLACE ST

HILLVIEW RD

BANNOCK DR

HILTON TER

KING

Playing Field

Depot

MOSS

QUEEN ST

STREET

ROAD

A905

Fallin

STIRLING ROAD

South Cockspow

Newmills

Dykes

STATION ROAD

Redhall

BANNOCKBURN ROAD

STATION ROAD

NNOCKBURN

Site of Battle of Bannockburn 24th June 1314

Skeoch

A91

Muirton

MUIRTON RD

Loanhead

RETAIL PARK

Depot

Works

MUNRO RD

A905

KERSE ROAD

GLEN TER

KERSE ROAD

ROAD

Cattle Market

TIP (disused)

MILLHALL

PIKE ROAD

MAR CRES

ROAD

Sewage Works

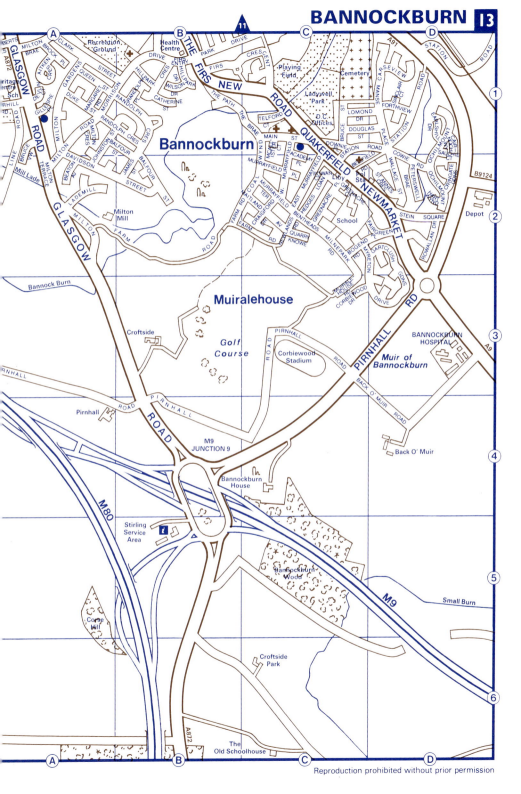

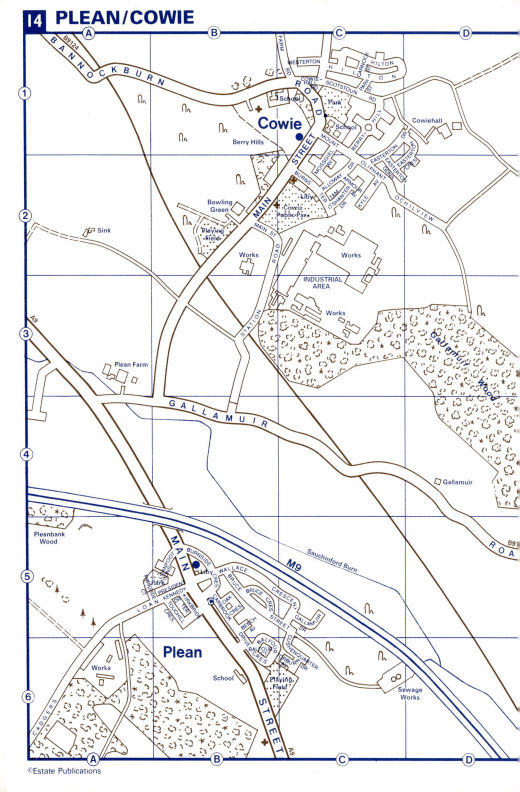

14 PLEAN/COWIE

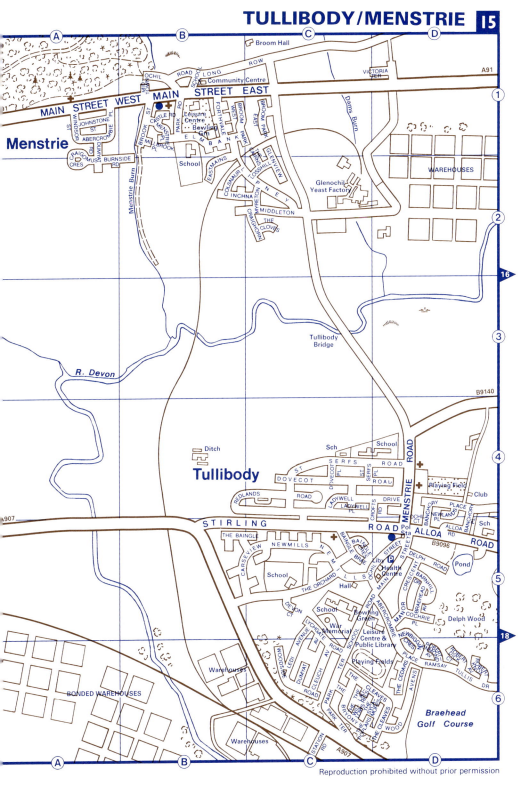

Menstrie

Tullibody

Glenochil
Yeast Factory

Tullibody
Bridge

R. Devon

Braehead
Golf Course

BONDED WAREHOUSES

WAREHOUSES

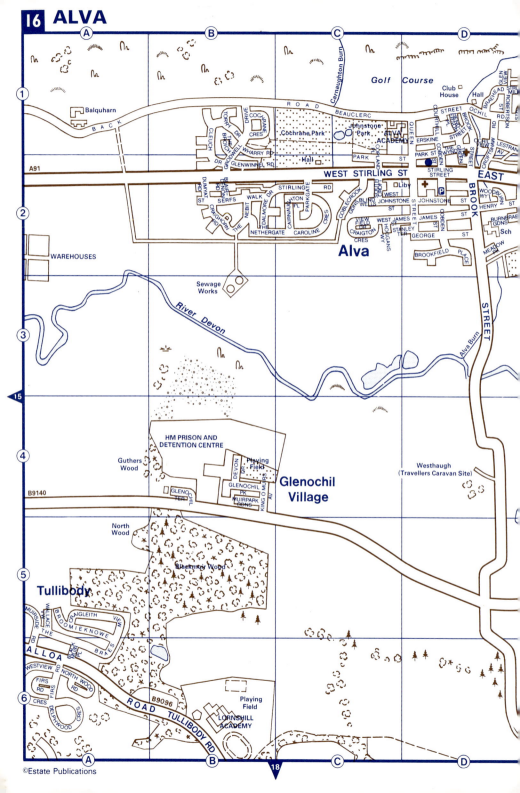

Golf Course

Club House

Hall

Balquharn

BACK ROAD BEAUCLERC

Carnaughton Burn

A91

Cochrane Park

Johnstone Park

ALVA ACADEMY

Cochrane Cres

WHARRY RD

Glenwinnel RD

Hall

WEST STIRLING ST

STIRLING STREET

EAST

QUEEN STREET

COURTHILL STREET

OCHIL STREET

BROOK STREET

VIEW STREET

CROFTSHAW AV

ERSKINE

PARK ST

STEWART

Liby

WEST

JOHNSTONE ST

JOHNSTONE ST

HENRY ST

WOODBURN WY

BRAEHEAD GLEN

ROBERTSON RD

LESTRAN

WEST JAMES ST

JAMES ST

COBDEN ST

BURNBRAE GDNS

Sch

MEADOW

WAREHOUSES

VIEW FIELD

CRAIGTON CRES

STANLEY TER

GEORGE ST

BROOKFIELD PLACE

Alva

HOGANS WY

Sewage Works

River Devon

15

Alva Burn

HM PRISON AND DETENTION CENTRE

Guthers Wood

Playing Field

DEVON DR

Glenochil Village

Westhaugh (Travellers Caravan Site)

B9140

GLENO TER

GLENOCHIL PK

MUIRPARK GDNS

KING O MUIRS AV

North Wood

Blackfaulds Wood

Tullibody

CRAIGLEITH VIEW

BROOMIEKNOWE

THE BRAES

MUIRSIDE RD

WALLACE RD

ALLOA

WESTVIEW RD

FIRS RD

NORTH WOOD RD

FIRS RD

FIRS CRES

DELPHWOOD CRES

B9096 ROAD TULLIBODY RD

Playing Field

LORNSHILL ACADEMY

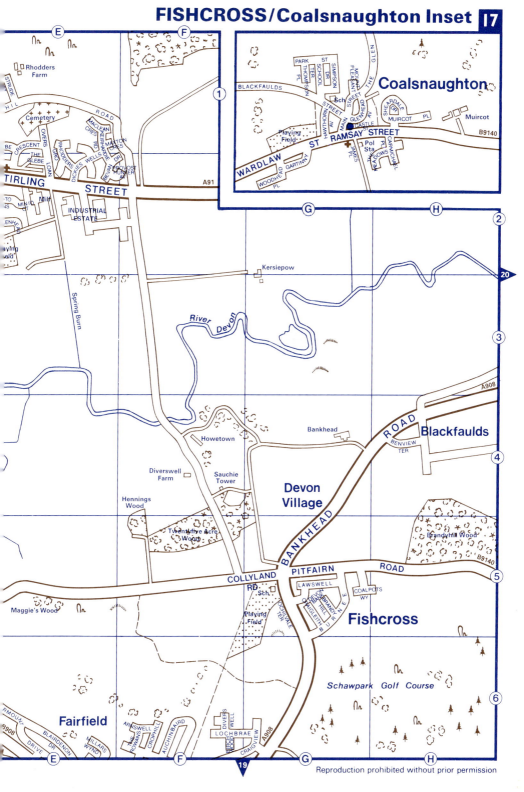

Rhodders Farm

Cemetery

STIRLING STREET

INDUSTRIAL ESTATE

Spring Burn

Kersiepow

River Devon

Coalsnaughton

BLACKFAULDS

PARK TER THOMPSON PL
SCHOOL DR
SIMPSON ST

MONT PLEASANT
THE GLEN

Sch

NORTHLAWN
STREET
MAIN STREET
GLENHEAD
CASTLE
SHEARDALE AV
MUIRCOT PL

Muircot

B9140

Playing Field

RAMSAY STREET

Pol Sta

WARDLAW ST

GARTINN

JAMES PL
CARMICHAEL
MEADOWS

WOODHEAD PL

A91

Howetown

Bankhead

Diverswell Farm

Sauchie Tower

Hennings Wood

Twentyfive Acre Wood

BENVIEW TER

ROAD

Blackfaulds

A908

Brandyhill Wood

B9140

Devon Village

BANKHEAD

COLLYLAND RD
Sth

PITFAIRN ROAD

LAWSWELL

CALEDON
BRANDY HILL
LANGLEITH BURNEE

COALPOTS WY

Fishcross

Maggie's Wood

Playing Field

LOCHINLATER

Fairfield

PARMOUNT DRIVE
BLAIRDENON DR
THE ROWANS
ARKSWELL
CROPHILL
AUCHINBAIRD
MILLARS WYND

LOCHDIVERS WELL
LOCHBRAE
CRAIGVIEW

FIRSH ROAD

A908

Schawpark Golf Course

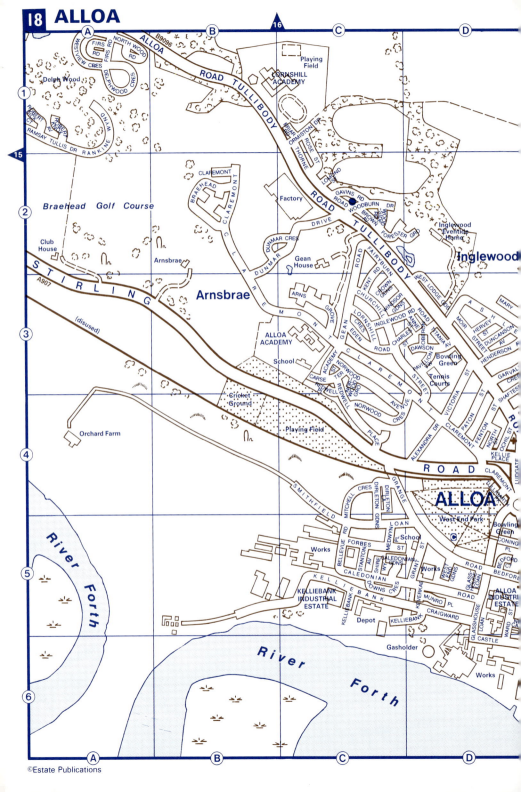

18 ALLOA

Delph Wood

Braehead Golf Course

Club House

Arnsbrae

STIRLING ROAD A907

(disused)

Orchard Farm

ALLOA ROAD TULLIBODY

ORMSHILL ACADEMY

Playing Field

Factory

Gean House

DUNMAR CRES

Arnsbrae

ALLOA ACADEMY

School

Cricket Ground

Playing Field

ROAD TULLIBODY

Inglewood Eventide Home

Inglewood

Bowling Green

Tennis Courts

Bowling Green

ALLOA

West End Park

SMITHFIELD

Orchard Farm

School

Works

CALEDONIAN

KELLIEBANK INDUSTRIAL ESTATE

Works

Depot

ALLOA INDUSTRIAL ESTATE

River Forth

River Forth

Gasholder

Works

©Estate Publications

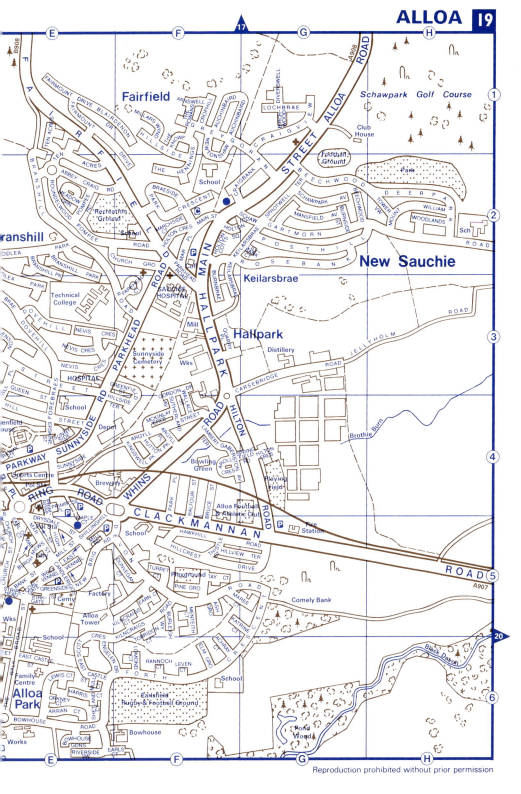

Schawpark Golf Course

Club House

Fairfield

Park

DEER PARK

School

WOODLANDS

Sch

New Sauchie

Keilarsbrae

Technical College

SAUCHIE HOSPITAL

Recreation Ground

School

Mill

Hallpark

Distillery

HOSPITAL

Sunnyside Cemetery

Wks

School

Depot

Bowling Green

Brothie Burn

Sports Centre

Brewery

Playing Field

Alloa Football & Athletic Club

Fire Station

RING ROAD

CLACKMANNAN ROAD

School

Hawkhill

Playground

Factory

Comely Bank

Alloa Tower

Black Devon

School

Family Centre

Alloa Park

Earnsfield Rugby & Football Ground

Pond Woods

Bowhouse

Works

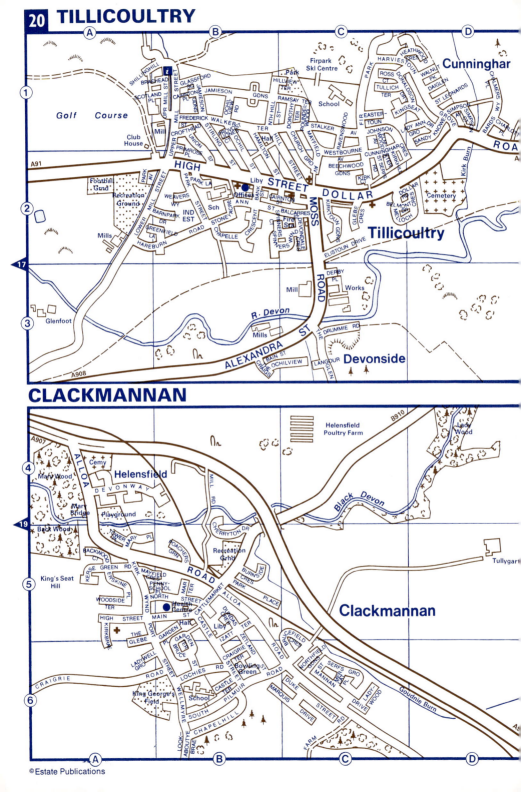

20 TILLICOULTRY

Cunninghar

Tillicoultry

Devonside

Golf Course

Club House

A91

Football Grand

Recreation Ground

Mills

Glenfoot

A908

Firpark Ski Centre

Park

School

Cemetery

Liby
Offices
Sch
Fire Stn

Mill

Works

R. Devon

Mills

CLACKMANNAN

Helensfield

Clackmannan

Helensfield Poultry Farm

B910

Lady Wood

A907

Mary Wood

Cemy

Back Wood

Mary Bridge

Playground

King's Seat Hill

Recreation Grnd

Health Centre

Hall

Liby

Bowling Green

King George's Field

School

Tullygar...

Goudnie Burn

Black Devon

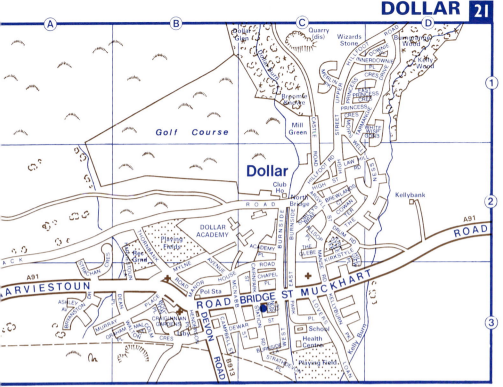

Reproduction prohibited without prior permission

A - Z INDEX TO STREETS
with Postcodes

The Index includes some names for which there is insufficient space on the maps. These names are preceded by an * and are followed by the nearest adjoining thoroughfare.

STIRLING

Abbey Mill, FK8	9 G5	
Abbey Rd. FK8	9 F4	
Abbey Rd Pl. FK8	9 F5	
Abbey Vw. FK9	9 G1	
Abbot Rd. FK7	11 G3	
*Abbotsford Pl,		
Millar Pl. FK8	9 F4	
Abercromby Dri. FK9	7 E3	
Abercromby Pl. FK8	3 B5	
Aboyne Av. FK9	9 G1	
Academy Pl. FK7	13 C2	
Academy Rd. FK8	3 B4	
Achray Dri. FK9	9 E2	
Adamson Pl. FK9	9 E2	
Afton Ct. FK7	11 F2	
Airth Dri. FK7	11 F3	
Airthrey Av. FK9	7 E5	
Airthrey Rd. FK9	7 F5	
Aitken Cres. FK7	11 F6	
Albert Pl. FK8	3 A5	
Albert St. FK15	5 C5	
Alexander Dri. FK9	6 D3	
Alexandra Pl. FK8	9 F4	
Allan Pk. FK8	3 C6	
Allan Wk. FK9	6 C3	
Allansvale Rd. FK9	6 D3	

Allanwater Gdns. FK9	7 E3	
Allanwood Ct. FK9	7 E3	
Alloa Rd. FK9	9 G1	
Alloway Dri. FK7	14 C2	
Almond Ct. FK7	11 F2	
Anchorscross. FK15	4 B4	
Anderson Clo. FK7	10 D3	
Anderson Cres. FK15	4 C4	
Anderson St. FK15	4 C4	
Anne Av. FK9	7 E4	
Anne St. FK15	4 C4	
Annfield Dri. FK7	11 F2	
Annfield Gdns. FK8	11 E2	
Annfield Gro. FK8	11 E2	
Arbroath Cres. FK9	9 F1	
Arcade. FK8	3 C5	
Archers Av. FK7	11 G4	
Ardoch Cres. FK7	4 C4	
Argyle Gro. FK15	5 C5	
Argyle Pk. FK15	5 B5	
Argyle Ter. FK15	5 B5	
Argyle Way. FK15	5 B5	
Argyll Av. FK8	3 D2	
Armour Av. FK7	14 C2	
Ash Ter. FK8	10 C3	
Ashbrae Gdns. FK7	11 E5	
Atholl Ct. FK15	4 C4	
Atholl Pl,		
Dunblane. FK15	4 C4	
Atholl Pl, Stirling. FK8	8 C3	
Auchinlay Rd. FK15	4 B3	
Avenue Pk. FK9	6 D3	
Back o' Dykes Rd. FK9	7 D4	
Back o' Hill Rd. FK8	3 A2	
Back o' Muir Rd. FK7	13 C3	
Back Wk. FK8	3 B4	
Backcroft. FK15	4 D3	
Baillie Waugh Rd. FK7	11 F4	

Baker St. FK8	3 B4	
Balfour Ct. FK7	14 B6	
Balfour Cres. FK8	14 B6	
Balfour St,		
Bannockburn. FK7	13 A1	
Balfour St, Stirling. FK8	8 C3	
Ballater Dri. FK9	9 F1	
Ballengeich Pass FK8	3 A2	
Ballengeich Rd. FK8	3 A2	
Balmoral Ct. FK15	5 C5	
Balmoral Pl. FK8	3 A5	
Balquhidderock. FK7	11 G4	
Balure Cres. FK7	12 F2	
Bandeath Rd. FK7	12 F3	
Bank St. FK8	3 C4	
Bannock Rd. FK7	12 E2	
Bannockburn Rd,		
Cowie. FK7	14 A1	
Bannockburn Rd,		
St Ninians. FK7	11 E4	
Bannockburn		
Station Rd. FK7	12 C3	
Barbour Av. FK7	11 G4	
Barn Rd. FK8	3 B3	
Barnsdale Rd. FK7	10 D5	
Barnton St. FK8	3 C3	
Barnwell Dri. FK9	9 F1	
Barony Ct. FK7	10 A2	
Batterflatts Gdns. FK7	10 C2	
Baxter St. FK7	12 F3	
Baxters Loan. FK15	5 A5	
Bayne St. FK8	3 C2	
Bearside Rd. FK7	10 D5	
Beaton Av. FK7	13 A2	
Beatty Av. FK8	8 D3	
Beda Pl. FK7	12 E2	
Beech Av. FK7	14 B5	
Beech La. FK9	9 F1	

Beech Rd. FK15	4 D4	
Bellfield Rd,		
Bannockburn. FK7	13 C2	
Bellfield Rd,		
St Ninians. FK7	11 E3	
Bentheads. FK7	13 C2	
Benview. FK7	11 F5	
Berkeley St. FK7	10 D3	
Berryhill. FK7	14 C1	
Birch Av. FK8	10 C3	
Birkhill Rd. FK7	10 B2	
Bishops Gdns. FK15	4 C4	
Blairforkie Dri. FK9	6 C2	
Bogend Rd. FK7	13 C2	
Bogside. FK15	4 D3	
Bohun Ct. FK7	11 G4	
Borestone Ct. FK7	11 E5	
Borestone Cres. FK7	11 E4	
Borestone Pl. FK7	11 E5	
Borrowlea Rd. FK7	11 F1	
Borrowmeadow Rd. FK7	9 G6	
Braehead Rd. FK7	11 F5	
Braemar Av. FK15	5 B5	
Braemar Gro. FK15	5 B5	
Braemar Pk. FK15	5 B5	
Braeport. FK15	4 D4	
Brentham Av. FK8	11 E2	
Brentham Cres. FK8	11 E2	
Bridge End. FK15	4 C4	
Bridgehaugh Rd. FK9	9 E3	
Broad St. FK8	3 B4	
Broadleys Rd. FK7	9 G6	
Brock Pl. FK7	11 F5	
Broom Ct. FK7	11 F4	
Broom Rd. FK7	11 F3	
Broomhill Pl. FK7	10 B1	
Broomridge Rd. FK7	11 F5	
Brown Av. FK9	9 F3	

Bruce Av. FK15	4 B4	
Bruce Cres. FK7	14 B5	
Bruce Dri. FK7	12 F2	
Bruce St,		
Bannockburn. FK7	13 C1	
Bruce St, Plean. FK7	14 B5	
Bruce St, Stirling. FK8	3 C2	
Bruce Ter. FK7	10 B2	
Bruce Vw. FK7	11 E6	
Buccleuth Ct. FK15	4 C3	
Buchan Dri. FK15	4 B4	
Buchanan Dri. FK9	9 F2	
Buntine Cres. FK7	10 D4	
Burghmuir Rd,		
St Ninians. FK7	11 E4	
Burghmuir Rd,		
Stirling. FK8	3 C2	
Burn Dri. FK7	11 F3	
Burns St. FK8	9 E3	
Burnside Cres. FK7	14 B5	
Burnside St. FK7	11 F1	
Cadgers Loan. FK7	14 A1	
Cairnoch Way. FK7	13 D1	
Calder Ct. FK7	11 F3	
Caledonian Pl. FK15	4 C4	
Calton Cres. FK7	11 E3	
Cameronian St. FK8	3 D6	
Campbell Ct. FK7	10 D4	
Canavan Ct. FK7	11 F4	
Carbrook Dri. FK7	14 B5	
Carlie Av. FK9	7 E5	
Carmichael Ct. FK9	7 E4	
Carnock St. FK7	14 C1	
Carrick Ct. FK7	11 F3	
Carron Pl. FK7	11 E5	
Carse of Lecropt Rd. FK9	6 A6	
Carseview. FK7	13 D1	
Castle Ct. FK8	3 B3	

Castle Rd. FK9 9 F2	Douglas Ter. FK7 10 B1	Gordon Cres, Stirling. FK8 8 C3	Kersebonny Rd. FK7 10 A1	Milton Gdns. FK7 11 F6
Castle Wynd. FK8 3 B4	Doune Rd. FK15 4 A3	Gowanhill Gdns. FK8 3 A1	Kilbryde Ct. FK15 4 C4	Milton Rd. FK7 11 F6
Castlevale. FK9 8 D1	Dowan Pl. FK7 10 B1	Gracie Cres. FK7 12 F3	Kilbryde Cres. FK15 4 B3	Milton Ter. FK7 11 F6
Castleview Dri. FK9 6 D4	Downie Pl. FK7 13 C1	Graham Av. FK9 9 G1	Kilbryde Gro. FK15 4 C3	Mine Rd. FK9 7 E3
Catherine St. FK7 13 B1	Drip Rd. FK8 3 B1	Graham St. FK9 7 E4	King St, Fallin. FK7 12 E2	Modan Rd. FK7 10 D4
Cauldhame Cres. FK7 10 A2	Drummond Pl. FK8 10 D1	Grampian Rd. FK9 10 B2	King St, Stirling. FK8 3 C5	Montgomery Way. FK9 9 E2
Causewayhead Rd. FK8 3 C1	Drummond Pl La. FK8 10 D1	Grange Gdns. FK9 7 F4	Kings Park Rd. FK8 3 B6	Montrose Rd. FK9 9 F2
Cawder Gdns. FK9 6 C3	Drummond Rise. FK15 4 D4	Grant Dri. FK15 4 B3	Kingstables La. FK8 3 B3	Montrose Way. FK15 4 B3
Cawder Rd. FK9 6 C4	Drumpark St. FK7 11 E4	Grant Pl. FK9 9 E2	Kinnoull Av. FK15 4 B4	Morgan Ct. FK7 11 F4
Cawdor Cres. FK15 4 B4	Duff Cres. FK8 8 C4	Graystale Rd. FK7 10 D5	Kippendavie Av. FK15 4 E2	Morley Cres. FK7 11 E5
Cecil St. FK7 11 F2	Duke St. FK7 11 F6	Greenacre Ct. FK7 13 C2	Kippendavie La. FK15 4 E2	Morris Ter. FK8 3 C4
Cedar Av. FK8 10 C3	Dumbarton Rd. FK8 3 C5	Greenacre Pl. FK7 13 C2	Kippendavie Rd. FK15 4 E2	Morrison Dri. FK7 11 F6
Centenary Wk. FK9 6 D5	Dumyat Rd. FK9 9 F2	Greenwood Av. FK8 3 A4	Kirk St. FK15 4 D4	Moss Rd. FK7 12 F3
Chalton Ct. FK9 7 F4	Dundas Rd. FK9 9 E1	Grendon Ct. FK8 11 E2	Kirk Wynd. FK7 11 E3	Mossgiel Av. Cowie. FK7 14 C2
Chalton Rd. FK9 7 E3	Dunster Rd. FK9 9 F2	Grendon Gdns. FK8 10 D2	Kirkbridge Ter. FK7 14 B5	Mossgiel Av, Stirling. FK8 8 D3
*Charles Av, Queens Way. FK9 7 E4	Dunvegan Dri. FK9 9 F3	Grierson Cres. FK7 10 A2	Kyle Av. FK7 14 C2	Mount Oliphant. FK7 14 C1
Charles Rodger Pl. FK7 7 E5	Dykedale. FK8 4 E4	Haig Av. FK8 9 E3	Laburnum Gro. FK8 10 D2	Mowbray Ct. FK7 14 C1
Charles St, Dunblane. FK15 5 C5	Earlsburn Av. FK7 10 D4	Haining. FK15 4 C3	Lademill. FK7 13 A2	Muiralehouse Rd. FK7 13 C3
Charles St, St Ninians. FK8 10 D2	Earlshill Dri. FK7 10 D4	Halberts Cres. FK7 11 E5	Ladysneuk Rd. FK9 9 G2	Muirend Rd. FK7 11 H1
Charter St. FK7 11 E5	East Murrayfield. FK7 13 C2	Haldane Av. FK9 7 E5	Laighhill Ct. FK15 4 D3	Muirton Rd. FK7 11 H1
Chartershall Rd. FK7 10 D5	Easter Cornton Rd. FK9 9 E1	Hamilton Dri. FK9 9 F1	Laighhill Pl. FK15 4 D3	Munro Av. FK9 9 E1
Chattan Av. FK9 9 E1	Easter Livilands. FK7 11 F3	Hanover Ct, Causewayhead. FK9 9 G1	Lamberton Av. FK7 11 F4	Munro Rd. FK7 11 H1
Chisholm Av, Cornton. FK9 9 E2	Eastertons Cres. FK7 14 C2	Hanover Ct, Dunblane. FK15 5 C5	Lamont Cres. FK7 12 F2	Murdoch Ter. FK15 4 B4
Chisholm Av, Dunblane. FK15 4 D3	Easterton Dri. FK7 14 C2	Hardie Ct. FK7 11 F4	Landrick Av. FK15 4 E2	Murnin Ct. FK7 11 F4
Churchill Dri. FK9 6 D5	Easterton Gdns. FK7 14 C2	Hardie Cres. FK7 12 E2	Laurelhill Gdns. FK8 10 D2	Murray Pl, Cambusbarron. FK7 10 A2
Claremont Dri. FK9 7 F3	Easton Ct. FK8 9 E3	Hart Wynd. FK7 13 D2	Laurelhill Pl. FK8 10 D2	Murray Pl, Stirling. FK8 3 C4
Clarendon Pl, Dunblane. FK15 5 C5	Edward Av. FK8 9 F4	Harvey Wynd. FK8 3 B2	Laurencecroft Rd. FK8 3 C1	Murrayfield Pl. FK7 13 C2
Clarendon Pl, Stirling. FK8 3 B6	Edward Pl. FK15 5 C5	Haugh Rd. FK9 9 E3	Ledi /w. FK9 9 E2	Murrayfield Ter. FK7 13 C2
Clarendon Rd. FK8 3 B5	Edward Rd. FK8 3 D2	Hawthorn Cres, Fallin. FK7 12 F3	Leewood Pk. FK15 5 E5	Murrayshall Rd. FK7 11 F5
Clark St. FK7 11 E5	Edward St. FK15 5 C5	Hawthorn Cres, Stirling. FK8 8 D3	Leewood Rd. FK15 5 E5	Myreton Dri. FK7 13 D2
Claymore Dri. FK9 11 G4	Elgin Dri. FK7 11 F4	Hawthorn Dri. FK7 12 E2	Leighton Av. FK15 4 F4	Nailer Rd. FK7 11 E5
Cleuch Rd. FK9 9 F2	Elizabeth St. FK8 10 D2	Hayford Pl. FK7 10 B2	Leighton Ct. FK15 4 F4	Nelson Pl. FK7 11 F1
Clifford Rd. FK8 11 E2	Elm St. FK8 8 C4	Hazelbank Gdns. FK8 8 D3	Lennox Av. FK7 11 E3	New Line Rd. FK7 11 E6
Coal Wynd. FK7 13 C2	Elmbank Rd. FK7 10 D5	Hedges Loan. FK7 13 C2	Linden Av. FK7 11 F1	New Rd. FK7 13 B1
Coldstream Av. FK15 4 B4	Endrick Pl. FK7 10 D4	Henderson St. FK9 6 D3	Lindsay Dri. FK9 9 E1	New St. FK9 6 D3
Colliers Rd. FK7 12 F3	Etive Pl. FK9 9 E2	Henry Milne Wk. FK9 7 H5	Lister Ct. FK9 6 D5	Newhouse. FK8 11 E3
Colquhoun St. FK7 11 F1	Ewing Ct. FK7 11 F4	Hermitage Rd. FK9 7 G5	Livilands Ct. FK8 11 E2	Newlands Rd. FK7 13 C2
Coney Pk. FK7 10 C1	Fairgreen Pl. FK7 13 D2	High St. FK15 4 D4	Livilands Gate. FK8 11 E2	Newmarket. FK7 13 D2
Coneyhill Rd. FK9 7 E4	Fairhill Rd. FK7 11 F6	Highfields. FK15 5 B5	Livilands La. FK8 11 E2	Newpark Cres. FK7 10 D5
Constable Rd. FK7 11 F2	Farm Rd, Bannockburn. FK7 13 C2	Hill St. FK7 11 E4	Loanfoot Gdns. FK7 14 B5	Newpark Rd. FK7 11 E5
Coppermine Pth. FK7 7 E3	Farm Rd, Cowie. FK7 14 C1	Hillfoots Rd. FK9 9 G1	Logie La. FK9 7 F4	Newton Cres. FK15 4 E3
Corbiewood Dri. FK7 13 C3	Farm Rd, Fallin. FK7 12 F2	Hillpark Cres. FK7 13 B1	Logie Rd. FK9 9 G1	Newton Loan. FK15 4 D4
Corn Exchange Rd. FK8 3 C5	Ferguson St. FK8 8 D3	Hillpark Dri. FK7 13 B1	Lomond Cres. FK9 9 E1	North End Rd. FK7 10 B2
Cornhill Cres. FK7 11 E4	*Ferndene Ter, New Rd. FK7 13 B1	Hillside Av. FK15 5 C5	Lomond Dri. FK7 13 C1	North St. FK9 9 G4
Cornton Cres. FK9 6 D5	Ferniebank Brae. FK9 6 C2	Hillview Dri. FK9 7 E4	Lothian Cres. FK9 9 F1	Oak Cres. FK7 14 B5
Cornton Rd, Bridge of Allan. FK9 6 D4	Ferry Orchard. FK9 9 G4	Hillview Pl. FK7 12 E2	Lovers Walk. FK8 3 C1	Oak Dri. FK7 12 F2
Cornton Rd, Cornton. FK9 9 E2	Ferry Rd. FK9 9 G4	Hilton. FK7 14 C1	Lower Bridge St. FK8 3 C1	Oak St. FK8 8 C4
Cowane St. FK8 3 C2	Firpark Ter. FK7 10 A2	Hilton Ter. FK7 12 E3	Lower Castlehill. FK8 3 B3	Ochil Cres. FK8 9 E3
Cowie Rd. FK7 13 D2	Firs Cres. FK7 11 G5	Hirst Cres. FK7 12 F3	Lyon Cres. FK9 6 D4	Ochil Rd. FK9 9 F1
Cowiehall Rd. FK7 14 C1	Firs Entry. FK7 11 G5	Holme Hill Ct. FK15 4 D4	McAlley Ct. FK9 6 D4	Ochil St. FK7 12 E2
Coxburn Brae. FK9 6 D1	Fishers Grn. FK9 6 D1	Hope St. FK8 8 C4	McAllister Ct. FK7 13 C1	Ochilmount. FK7 13 D2
Coxhill Rd. FK7 10 D4	Forglen Cres. FK9 7 E5	Hopetoun Dri. FK9 6 D3	Macdonald Dri. FK7 10 D4	Ochiltree. FK15 4 E3
Craig Ct. FK9 7 E5	Forglen Rd. FK9 7 E5	Howlands Rd. FK7 10 D5	McGrigor Rd. FK7 11 E4	Ochiltree Ct. FK15 4 E4
Craig Cres. FK9 9 G2	Forrest Rd. FK8 3 D2	Hume Ct. FK9 7 E5	McLachlan Av. FK7 11 E5	Ochilview. FK7 14 C2
Craig Leith Rd. FK7 11 G2	Forth Ct. FK8 3 D2	Hume Cres. FK9 6 D4	McLaren Ter. FK7 11 E5	Ochlochy Pk. FK15 4 D4
Craigend Rd. FK7 10 D4	Forth Cres. FK8 3 D3	Huntley Cres. FK8 8 C3	McPherson Dri. FK8 8 D3	Ogilvie Pl. FK9 6 D5
Craigford Dri. FK7 13 C2	Forth Pl, Bridge of Allan. FK9 6 D6	INDUSTRIAL ESTATES:	Mace Ct. FK7 11 H4	Ogilvie Rd. FK8 10 D2
Craigforth Cres. FK8 8 C4	Forth Pl, Stirling. FK8 3 D3	Back o'Hill Ind Est. FK8 3 A1	Main St. Cambusbarron. FK7 10 A2	Old Doune Rd. FK15 4 B4
Craighall St. FK8 8 C3	Forth St, Fallin. FK7 12 E2	Broadleys Ind Est. FK7 11 G2	Main St, Bannockburn. FK7 13 C1	Old Drove Rd. FK7 10 A2
Cringate Gdns. FK7 13 D2	Forth St, Stirling. FK8 3 D2	Castle Business Pk. FK8 8 B3	Main St, Cowie. FK7 14 C1	Old Military Rd. FK9 6 C3
Crofthead Ct. FK8 3 B3	Forthview, Bannockburn. FK7 13 D1	Springkerse Ind Est. FK7 11 G1	Main St, Plean. FK7 14 B5	Orchard Rd. FK9 6 D5
Crofthead Rd. FK8 3 B3	Forthview, Stirling. FK8 9 E4	Stirling Enterprise Pk. FK7 11 F2	Main St, St Ninians. FK7 11 E4	Park Av. FK8 3 B6
Cromlix Cres. FK15 4 B4	Fountain Rd. FK9 6 D4	Thistle Ind Est. FK7 11 F1	Maitland Av. FK7 13 C2	Park Cres. FK7 11 G5
Cruachan Av. FK9 9 E2	Fraser Pl. FK9 9 E1	Inverallan Ct. FK9 6 C3	Maitland Cres. FK7 11 E5	Park Dri. FK7 11 G5
Crum Cres. FK7 11 F5	Friars St. FK8 3 C5	Inverallan Dri. FK9 6 C4	Manse Cres. FK7 11 E3	Park Gdns. FK7 11 G5
Cultenhove Cres. FK7 10 D4	Gallamuir Dri. FK7 14 C5	Inverallan Rd. FK9 6 C4	Manse P!. FK7 13 D1	Park La. FK8 3 C3
Cultenhove Pl. FK7 10 D4	Gallamuir Rd. FK7 14 B4	Irvine Pl. FK8 3 B3	Mar Pl. FK8 3 B3	Park Pl. FK7 10 C1
Cultenhove Rd. FK7 10 D4	Gambeson Cres. FK7 11 G4	Ivanhoe Pl. FK8 8 D3	Margaret Rd. FK7 11 F6	Park St. FK7 14 C1
Cunningham Rd. FK9 11 G1	Gartclush Gdns. FK7 13 D2	Jail Wynd. FK8 3 B4	Marlborough Dri. FK9 9 F2	Park Ter. FK8 3 B6
Cushenquarter Dri. FK7 14 C4	Gateside Rd. FK7 10 D5	James St, Bannockburn. FK7 13 B2	Marschall Ct. FK7 11 G4	Parkdyke. FK7 10 B1
Dalgleish Ct. FK8 3 C6	George St. FK15 5 C5	James St, Stirling. FK8 3 D2	Maurice Av. FK7 11 G3	Parkside Ct. FK7 14 A5
Dalmorglen Pk. FK7 10 C2	Gillespie Pl. FK7 11 F6	John Murray Dri. FK9 6 D3	Maxwell Pl. FK8 3 C4	Paterson Pl. FK9 7 E5
Dargai Ter. FK15 4 C3	Gillies Dri. FK7 11 F3	John R. Gray Rd. FK15 5 C5	Mayfield Ct. FK7 11 E4	Pathfoot Av. FK9 7 F4
Darn Rd, Bridge of Allan. FK9 6 C2	Gillies Hill. FK7 10 A2	Johnson Av. FK9 9 E2	Mayfield St. FK7 11 E4	Pathfoot Dri. FK9 7 F4
Darn Rd, Dunblane. FK15 5 D5	Gladstone Pl. FK8 11 E1	Johnston St. FK7 13 A1	Mayne Av. FK8 9 F4	Pelstream Av. FK7 11 F3
Darnley St. FK8 3 B4	Glaive Av. FK7 11 G4	Keir Av. FK8 9 E3	Meadow Pl. FK8 9 F4	Pendreich Rd. FK9 6 D2
Davidson St. FK7 13 A2	Glasgow Rd. FK7 11 E4	Keir Ct. FK9 7 E4	Meadowforth Rd. FK7 11 F1	Pendreich Way. FK9 7 G5
Dean Cres. FK8 3 D2	Glebe Av. FK8 3 B6	Keir Gdns. FK9 6 D4	Meadowland Rd. FK9 7 E4	Perth Rd. FK15 4 D4
Dermoch Dri. FK15 4 B4	Glebe Cres. FK8 3 B6	Keir Gdns. FK9 9 E2	Melfort Dri. FK7 11 F3	Peterswell Brae. FK7 13 D2
Deroran Pl. FK8 10 C2	Glebe Pl. FK15 4 C4	Keir La. FK15 5 E5	Melville Pl. FK9 7 E4	Pike Rd. FK7 11 G3
Devlin Ct. FK7 11 E6	Glen Ct. FK15 4 E4	Keir St: Bridge of Allan. FK9 6 D4	Melville Ter. FK8 3 C6	Pirnhall Rd. FK7 13 C3
Donaldson Pl. FK7 10 B2	Glen Rd, Bridge of Allan. FK9 6 D2	Keir St, Dunblane. FK15 4 C4	Mentieth Rd. FK8 9 E2	Pitt Ter. FK8 3 C6
Douglas Dri. FK7 11 G4	Glen Rd, Dunblane. FK15 4 D4	Keith Av. FK7 11 F4	Mentieth Vw. FK15 4 E3	Polmaise Av. FK7 11 E4
Douglas St, Bannockburn. FK7 13 C1	Glen Tye Rd. FK7 11 G2	Kelly Ct. FK8 3 B4	Menzies Dri. FK8 8 D3	Polmaise Cres. FK7 12 E2
Douglas St, Stirling. FK8 3 C2	Glencairn St. FK7 11 F4	Kenilworth Ct. FK9 7 F4	Middlemuir Rd. FK7 11 F1	Polmaise Rd. FK7 10 C3
	Glencoe Rd. FK8 3 B2	Kenilworth Rd. FK9 7 F4	Mill Ct. FK15 4 C3	Port St. FK8 3 C6
	Glendevon Dri. FK7 11 F5	Kenningknowes Rd. FK8 10 C2	Mill Rd. FK15 4 C3	Pottis Rd. FK7 11 G4
	Gogar St. FK7 11 F5	Kent Rd. FK7 11 F2	Mill Row. FK15 4 C4	President Kennedy Dri. FK7 14 B5
	Goosecroft Rd. FK8 3 C3	Kerse Rd. FK7 11 F1	Millar Pl. FK8 9 F4	Princes St. FK8 3 C4
	Gordon Cres, Bridge of Allan. FK9 6 D3		Millhall Rd. FK7 11 G3	Pullar Av. FK9 6 D5
			Milnepark Rd. FK7 13 C2	Pullar Ct. FK7 7 E5
			Milton. FK7 13 A2	Quakerfield. FK7 13 C1
			Milton Brae. FK7 11 E5	
			Milton Cres. FK7 13 A1	

Quarry Knowe. FK7 13 C2
Quarry Rd. FK7 10 A2
Queen St,
Bannockburn. FK7 11 F6
Queen St, Fallin. FK7 12 E3
Queen St, Stirling. FK8 3 C3
Queens Av. FK9 7 E4
*Queens Ct,
Queens La. FK9 6 D3
Queens La. FK9 6 D3
Queens Rd. FK8 3 A5
Queenshaugh Dri. FK8 9 F4
Ramsay Pl. FK8 3 B1
Randolph Ct. FK8 11 E2
Randolph Cres. FK7 13 A1
Randolph Pl. FK7 13 B1
Randolph Rd. FK8 11 E3
Randolph Ter. FK7 11 E3
Raploch Rd. FK8 8 C3
Raymoyle. FK15 4 D3
Ritchie Ct. FK5 4 C4
Riverbank Vw. FK8 9 F5
Riverside Dri. FK8 9 G4
Robertson Pl. FK7 11 E4
Roman Way. FK15 5 B5
Ronald Pl. FK8 3 D3
Rosebery Pl. FK8 3 D3
Rosebery Ter. FK8 3 D3
Ross Ct. FK7 11 F4
Roughburn Rd. FK9 7 E5
Rowallan Rd. FK7 13 D2
Rowan Ct. FK7 13 C2
Royal Gdns. FK8 3 A4
Ruskie Rd. FK9 9 E2
Rutherford Ct. FK9 6 D3
Rylands Av. FK15 4 E2
Rylands Rd. FK15 4 E2
St Annes Cres. FK7 13 D2
St Blanes Rd. FK15 4 D4
St Clement Av. FK5 5 B5
St James Cres. FK9 9 G4
St James Orch. FK9 9 G5
St John St. FK8 3 B4
St Laurence Av. FK15 5 B5
St Margarets Dri. FK15 4 E4
St Margarets Loan. FK15 4 E4
St Marys Ct. FK15 4 D4
St Marys Dri. FK15 4 D4
St Marys Wynd. FK8 3 B3
St Ninians Rd,
Cambusbarron. FK7 10 B2
St Ninians Rd,
Stirling. FK8 3 C6
St Thomas's Pl. FK7 10 B1
St Thomas's Well. FK7 10 B1
St Valery Ct. FK7 10 D3
St Valery Dri. FK7 10 D3
Sauchie Ct. FK7 13 D2
Schilton Way. FK7 11 G4
Scotstoun Rd. FK7 14 C1
Scott Dri. FK15 4 B4
Scott St. FK8 9 E3
Seaforth Pl. FK8 3 C4
Seton Ct. FK7 11 F4
Sheriffmuir Rd. FK9 7 F4
Sheriffmuirlands Rd. FK9 9 G2
Shiphaugh Pl. FK8 9 F4
Shirras Brae Rd. FK7 11 E3
Shore Rd. FK8 3 D4
Sinclair Ct. FK7 13 D1
Sinclair Dri. FK7 12 F3
Sinclairs St. FK15 4 D4
Smithy Loan. FK15 4 D4
Snowdon Pl. FK8 10 D1
Snowdon Pl La. FK8 10 D2
South St. FK9 9 G4
Southfield Cres. FK8 10 D1
Spey Ct. FK7 11 F3
Spittal Hill. FK9 7 G6
Spittal St. FK8 3 B4
Springbank Cres. FK15 4 C4
Springbank Gdns. FK15 4 B3
Springbank Rd. FK7 11 F1
Springfield Ct. FK15 4 C4
Springfield Dri. FK7 11 F2
Springfield Ter. FK15 4 C4
Springkerse Rd. FK7 11 F1
Springwood Av. FK7 10 C2
Stanley Dri. FK7 7 E4
Station Rd,
Bannockburn. FK7 13 C1
Station Rd,
Bridge of Allan. FK9 6 C3
Station Rd, Cowie. FK7 14 B3
Station Rd,
Dunblane. FK15 4 C4
Station Rd, Stirling. FK8 3 C5

Stein Sq. FK7 13 D2
Stevenson Ct. FK9 7 E5
Stewart Rd. FK9 6 C4
Stewart Sq. FK8 8 D3
Stewart St. FK7 10 B1
Stirling Rd. FK15 5 C5
Stirling Rd. FK7 12 D2
Strathallan Ct. FK9 6 D5
Strathallan Rd. FK9 6 D4
Strathmore Av. FK15 4 B3
Strathmore Cres. FK9 9 E2
Strathmore Dri. FK9 9 E2
Sunnybank Rd. FK7 11 E4
Sunnylaw Rd. FK9 6 D2
Sunnylaw Rd. FK9 7 E3
Sunnyside. FK7 11 E3
Sutherland Av. FK8 9 F4
Sycamore Pl. FK8 10 C3
Tam o'Shanter Dri. FK7 14 C2
Tannahill Ter. FK15 4 C3
Tannery La. FK8 3 C3
Telford Ct. FK7 13 C1
The Avenue. FK9 6 D3
The Brae,
Bannockburn. FK7 13 C1
The Brae,
Cambusbarron. FK7 10 A2
The Crescent. FK15 4 D4
The Cross. FK15 4 C4
The Firs. FK7 11 G5
The Homesteads. FK7 10 B1
The Path. FK7 13 B1
The Yetts. FK7 10 A2
Thistle Shopping
Centre. FK8 3 D5
Thomson Pl. FK7 10 A2
Torbrex. FK7 10 D3
Torbrex Farm Rd. FK7 10 D3
Torbrex Rd. FK7 10 C3
Torburn Av. FK7 14 C6
Touch Rd. FK7 14 B5
Touchill Cres. FK7 14 B5
Towers Pl. FK8 9 G1
Underwood Cotts. FK7 10 A2
*Underwood Rd,
St Ninians Rd. FK7 10 B2
Union St. FK8 3 C2
Upper Bridge St. FK8 3 B3
Upper Castlehill. FK8 3 B3
Upper Craigs. FK8 3 C6
Upper Glen Rd. FK9 6 D2
Vale Gro. FK9 6 D6
Valleyfield Pl. FK7 11 F1
Victoria Pl. FK8 3 A6
Victoria Rd. FK8 3 B5
Victoria Sq. FK8 3 A5
Viewfield St. FK8 3 C4
Voil Rd. FK9 9 E2
Vorlich Pl. FK9 9 E2
Wallace Cres. FK8 14 B5
Wallace Gdns. FK9 9 G2
Wallace Pl,
Cambusbarron. FK7 10 B3
Wallace Pl, Fallin. FK7 12 E2
Wallace Rd. FK15 4 B4
Wallace St,
Bannockburn. FK7 13 D2
Wallace St, Stirling. FK8 3 D3
Wallstale Rd. FK7 10 D4
Waverley Cres. FK8 9 F4
Weaver Row. FK7 11 E3
Weir Dri. FK7 12 F3
Well Pl. FK15 4 C4
Well Rd. FK9 6 D3
Wellgate Dri. FK9 7 F4
Wellgreen. FK8 3 C6
Wellgreen Rd. FK8 3 C6
Wellpark Cres. FK7 10 D3
Welsh Gdns. FK9 6 D3
West Murrayfield. FK7 13 C2
Westerlands Dri. FK8 11 E3
Westerlea Ct. FK9 6 D6
Westerlea Dri. FK9 6 D6
Westerton. FK7 14 C1
Westerton Dri. FK9 6 D4
Whins Rd. FK8 11 F5
Whinwell Rd. FK8 3 B3
Whitecross Av. FK15 4 E4
Whitehill Pl. FK8 10 D2
Whitehouse Rd. FK11 9 G1
Wier St. FK8 8 C3
Willam Booth Pl. FK7 10 D4
Williamfield Av. FK7 11 E3
Wilson Dri. FK7 13 B1
Windsor Dri. FK8 3 B6
Wishart Dri. FK7 11 G4
Woodside Ct. FK7 10 A2

Woodside Pl. FK7 12 E2
Woodside Rd. FK8 8 D3

ALLOA

Abbey Craig Rd. FK10 19 E2
Abercrombie Pl,
Menstrie. FK11 15 A1
Abercrombie Pl,
Tullibody. FK10 15 D5
Academy Pl. FK14 21 C2
Academy St. FK10 18 C3
Achray Ct. FK10 19 F6
Alexandra Dri. FK10 18 D4
Alexandra St. FK13 20 B3
Alloa Rd,
Clackmannan. FK10 20 A4
Alloa Rd,
New Sauchie. FK10 19 G1
Alloa Rd,
Tullibody. FK10 15 D5
Allsop Pl. FK14 21 C2
Ann St. FK13 20 B2
Anne St. FK10 18 D3
Argyll Pl. FK10 19 F4
Argyll St, Alloa. FK10 19 F4
Argyll St, Dollar. FK14 21 C2
Arns Gro. FK10 18 C3
Arnswell. FK10 19 F1
Aroll Cres. FK10 19 F4
Arran Ct. FK10 19 E6
*Arthur Bett Ct,
High St. FK13 20 C2
Ash Gro. FK10 19 F5
Ashley Av. FK14 21 A3
Ashley St. FK10 18 D3
Auchinbaird. FK10 19 F1
Back Rd, Alva. FK12 16 A1
Back Rd, Dollar. FK14 21 A3
Backwood Ct. FK10 20 A5
Bain St. FK13 20 B3
Baingle Brae. FK10 15 C5
Baingle Cres. FK10 15 C5
Balcarres St. FK13 20 C2
Balfour St. FK10 19 F4
Banchory Pl. FK10 15 D5
Bank St, Alloa. FK10 19 E5
Bank St,
Tillicoultry. FK13 20 B2
Bards Way. FK13 20 D1
Barnhill Dri. FK10 15 D5
Barnpark Dri. FK13 20 B2
Beauclerc St. FK12 16 C1
Bedford Ct. FK10 18 D5
Bedford Pl. FK10 18 D5
Beechwood. FK10 19 G2
Beechwood Gdns. FK13 20 C2
Bellevue Rd. FK10 18 C5
Belmont Dri. FK13 20 C2
Benview Ter. FK10 17 H4
Bevan Dri. FK12 17 E2
Birchwood. FK10 19 G1
Blackfaulds St. FK13 Inset 17
Blackmuir Pl. FK10 16 A6
Blairdenon Rd. FK12 16 B2
Blairdenon Dri. FK10 19 E1
Blindwells. FK12 16 C2
Bogton Pl. FK14 21 B3
Bowhouse Gdns. FK10 19 E6
Bowhouse Rd. FK10 19 E6
Braehead, Alva. FK12 16 D1
Braehead,
Arnsbrae. FK10 18 B2
Braehead,
Tillicoultry. FK13 20 B1
Braehead Av. FK10 15 D5
Braeside. FK10 19 F2
Brandy Hill. FK13 17 G5
Branshill Pk FK10 19 E2
Branshill Rd. FK10 19 E2
Brewlands Ct. FK14 21 C2
Briar Rd. FK10 18 C1
Bridge St. FK14 21 C3
Broad St. FK10 19 E6
Brook St, Alva. FK12 16 D2
Brook St,
Menstrie. FK11 15 B1
Brookfield Pl. FK10 16 D2
Broom Pk East. FK11 15 C1
Broom Pk West. FK11 15 B1
Broomieknowe. FK10 16 A5
Brown Av. FK10 18 C2
Bruce St, Alloa. FK10 19 F4
Bruce St,
Clackmannan. FK10 20 B6

Brucefield Cres. FK10 20 C6
Bryanston Dri. FK14 21 A3
Burgh Mews. FK10 19 E5
Burleigh Way. FK10 19 F5
Burnbrae. FK10 19 F3
Burnbrae Gdns. FK12 16 D2
Burnee. FK10 17 G5
Burnside Cres. FK10 20 B5
Burnside La. FK14 21 C3
Burnside Rd. FK11 15 A1
Burnside St. FK10 19 G2
Cairnaughton Pl. FK12 16 C2
Cairnpark St. FK14 21 C3
Cairnton Pl. FK13 20 B1
Cairnton St. FK13 20 B3
Caledonian Gdns. FK10 18 C5
Caledonian Rd. FK10 18 C5
Campbell St. FK14 21 B3
Candleriggs. FK10 19 E5
Caroline Cres. FK12 16 C2
Carse Ter. FK10 18 C3
Carsebridge Rd. FK10 19 F3
Carseview. FK10 18 B5
*Castle Ct,
Castle Rd. FK11 15 B1
Castle Rd,
Menstrie. FK11 15 B1
Castle Rd, Dollar. FK14 21 C2
Castle St, Alloa. FK10 18 D6
Castle St,
Clackmannan. FK10 20 B5
Castle St,
Coalsnaughton. FK13 Inset 17
Castle Ter. FK10 20 B6
Cattlemarket. FK10 20 B5
Chalmers Pl. FK13 20 D1
Chapel Pl. FK14 21 C3
Chapelhill. FK10 20 B6
Chapelle Cres. FK13 20 B2
Charles St. FK10 18 C3
Charlotte Pl. FK13 20 D1
Cherryton Dri. FK10 20 B5
Church Gro, Alloa. FK10 19 E2
Church Gro,
Tillicoultry. FK13 20 C1
Church St. FK10 19 E5
Churchill St. FK10 18 C3
Clackmannan Rd. FK10 19 F4
Claremont, Alloa. FK10 18 D4
Claremont,
Arnsbrae. FK10 18 B2
Cleuch Av. FK10 15 C6
Cleuch Dri. FK12 16 B1
Coalgate. FK10 19 E5
*Coalpots Way. FK10 17 G5
Cobden St. FK12 16 D1
Cobden St. FK12 16 D2
Coblecrook Gdns. FK12 16 C2
Cochrane Cres. FK12 16 B1
Cochrie Pl. FK10 15 D5
*Colliers Ct,
Balcarres St. FK13 20 C2
Collyland Rd. FK10 17 F5
Colsnaur. FK11 15 B2
Coningsby Pl. FK10 18 D5
Copland Pl. FK12 16 C2
Courthill. FK12 16 D1
Cowan Ter. FK14 21 C2
Craigbank. FK10 19 F2
Craighorn. FK10 15 C2
Craighorn Rd. FK12 16 B2
Craiginnian Gdns. FK14 21 B3
Craigleith. FK10 17 G5
Craigleith Vw. FK10 16 A6
Craigomus Cres. FK11 15 A1
Craigrie Rd. FK10 20 A6
Craigrie Ter. FK10 20 B6
Craigton Cres. FK10 16 C2
Craigview. FK10 19 G1
Craigward. FK10 18 D5
Crofthead. FK13 20 B1
Crofts Rd. FK10 15 D4
Croftshaw Rd. FK12 16 D2
Crophill. FK10 19 F1
Crown Gdns. FK10 18 C3
Cunningham Dri. FK13 20 C2
Daiglen. FK13 20 D1
Dalmore Dri. FK12 16 B2
Dawson Av. FK10 18 D3
Dean Pl. FK14 21 B3
Deerpark. FK10 19 H2
Delph Rd. FK10 15 D5
Delphwood Cres. FK10 16 A6
Derby Pl. FK13 20 C3
Devon Bank. FK10 17 G5
Devon Ct. FK10 15 C5

Devon Dri. FK10 16 B4
Devon Rd, Alloa. FK10 19 F5
Devon Rd, Dollar. FK14 21 B3
Devondale Cres. FK13 20 C2
Devonway. FK10 20 A4
Dewar St. FK14 21 B3
Dickies Wells. FK12 17 E2
Dirleton Gdns. FK10 18 C4
Dirleton La. FK10 18 C4
Diverswell. FK10 19 G1
Dollar Rd. FK13 20 C2
Donaldson Dri. FK10 20 C1
Doo'Cot Brae. FK10 18 D3
Dorothy Ter. FK13 20 C1
Dovecot Pl. FK10 15 C4
Dovecot Rd. FK10 15 C4
Dovehill. FK10 19 E3
Downie Pl. FK14 21 D1
Downs Cres. FK10 18 C5
Drum Rd. FK14 21 C2
Drummie Rd. FK13 20 C3
Drysdale St. FK10 19 E5
Duke St. FK10 20 C6
*Duke St,
Beauclerc St. FK12 16 D1
Dumyat Av. FK10 15 C6
Dumyat Rd, Alva. FK12 16 B2
Dumyat Rd,
Menstrie. FK11 15 A1
Duncanson Av. FK10 18 D3
Dundas Cres. FK10 20 B5
Dunmar Cres. FK10 18 B2
Dunmar Dri. FK10 18 B2
Dunvegan Ct. FK10 19 F5
Earl of Mar Ct. FK10 19 E5
Earls Ct. FK10 19 E6
Earn Ct. FK10 19 F5
East Burnside. FK10 21 C3
East Castle St. FK10 19 E6
East Mains. FK11 15 B1
East Princess Cres. FK14 21 C1
East Stirling St. FK12 16 D2
East Vennel. FK10 19 E5
Eastertoun. FK13 20 C1
Eden Rd. FK10 18 C3
Elistoun Dri. FK13 20 C2
Elm Gro. FK10 19 F6
Elmbank. FK11 15 B1
Elmwood Av. FK13 20 C1
Engelen Dri. FK10 19 E6
Erskine Pl. FK10 20 A5
Erskine St, Alloa. FK10 19 E4
Erskine St, Alva. FK12 16 D1
Fairfield. FK10 19 E1
Fairmount Dri. FK10 19 E1
Fairyburn Rd. FK10 18 C2
Farm Rd. FK10 20 C6
Fenton St. FK10 18 D4
Fir Park. FK13 20 C1
Firs Rd. FK10 16 A6
Forbes St. FK10 18 C5
Forebraes. FK10 19 E4
Forester Gro. FK10 18 C2
Forth Cres. FK10 19 F6
Forthvale. FK11 15 B1
Frederick St. FK13 20 B1
Gaberston Av. FK10 19 F4
Garden Pl. FK10 20 B5
Garden Ter. FK10 20 B6
Gartinny. FK13 Inset 17
Gartmorn Rd. FK10 19 G2
Garvally Cres. FK10 18 D3
Gavins Rd. FK10 18 C2
Gean Rd. FK10 18 C3
George St. FK12 16 D2
Gibson Clo. FK14 21 C3
Glassford Sq. FK13 20 C3
Glasshouse Loan. FK10 18 D5
Glebe Cres, Alva. FK12 17 E1
Glebe Cres,
Tillicoultry. FK13 20 C2
Glebe Ter. FK10 19 E5
Glen View. FK12 16 D1
Glenhead Av. FK13 Inset 17
Glenochil Pk. FK10 16 B4
Glenochil Ter. FK10 16 B4
Glenview. FK11 15 C2
Glenwinnel Rd. FK12 16 B2
Gordon Dri. FK10 19 F3
Graham Pl. FK14 21 B3
Grange Rd. FK10 18 C4
Grant St. FK10 18 D5
Greenfield La. FK13 20 B2
Greenfield St. FK10 19 F3
Greenhead. FK12 16 D2
Greenside St. FK10 19 E5
Greygoran. FK10 19 F1